MACHINE MANIA

MOTORBIKES

Frances Ridley

WITHDRAWN

Copyright © ticktock Entertainment Ltd 2007
First published in Great Britain in 2007 by ticktock Media Ltd.,
Unit 2, Orchard Business Centre, North Farm Road,
Tunbridge Wells, Kent, TN2 3XF

ticktock project editor: Julia Adams
ticktock project designer: Emma Randall

We would like to thank: Alix Wood.

ISBN 978 1 84696 562 3

Printed in China
9 8 7 6 5 4 3 2

Picture credits:
b=bottom; c=centre; t=top; r=right; l=left
All images Car Photo Library - www.carphoto.co.uk, except: Action Plus: 15tr, 21tr;
Alvey and Towers: 20-21c, b/c cl

Every effort has been made to trace the copyright holders,
and we apologise in advance for any unintentional omissions.
We would be pleased to insert the appropriate acknowledgements
in any subsequent edition of this publication.

Contents

Aprilia RSV Mille R 4

Buell XB9R Firebolt 6

Honda CBR1100XX Blackbird 8

Kawasaki Ninja ZX-12R 10

Harley-Davidson V-Rod 12

Ducati 999S 14

MV Agusta F4 SPR Senna 16

Suzuki GSX1300R Hayabusa 18

Suzuki GSXR1000 20

Yamaha YZF-R1 22

Glossary 24

Aprilia RSV Mille R

The RSV Mille R was launched in 2002. The R stands for 'Racing'.

The Mille R is big, fast and comfortable to ride. It has a top speed of 270 km/h.

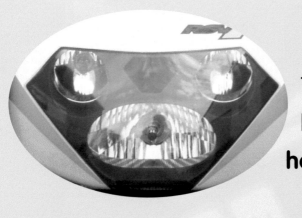

The Mille R
has a triple
headlight.

It also has special brakes
at the front. They are
much stronger than
normal brakes.

You can stop
very quickly if
you need to.

Buell XB9R Firebolt

The Firebolt is very light for a motorbike – it only weighs 175 kg.

Its powerful **engine** makes it very fast. It has a top speed of 209 km/h.

The Firebolt is an unusual bike. It has a hollow frame to store fuel.

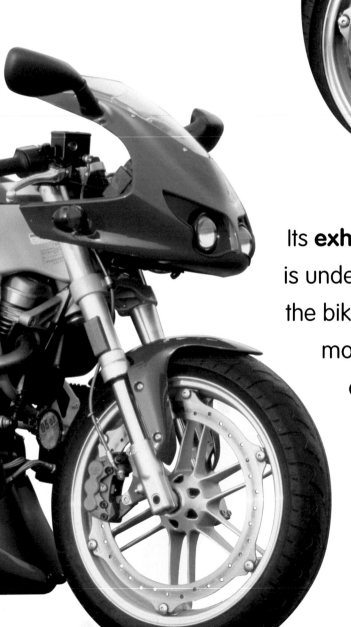

Its **exhaust** is underneath the bike. Most motorcycle exhausts are on the side.

Honda CBR1100XX Blackbird

The Blackbird has a huge **engine**.
It also has a streamlined shape.

It can race from 0 to 209 km/h in
just 11 seconds.

In 2001, a **turbo-charged** Blackbird did a wheelie at 321 km/h.

It has special brakes. They slow down the front and back tyres at the same time.

Kawasaki Ninja ZX-12R

The Ninja ZX-12R has a top speed of 305 km/h! Its smooth shape helps the bike go fast.

The Ninja has a scoop under the **headlight**. The scoop forces air into the **engine**. This drags in extra fuel and gives the Ninja more power.

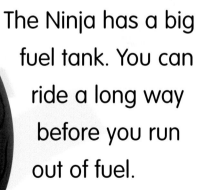

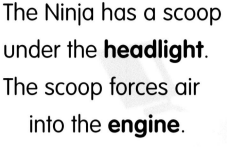

The Ninja has a big fuel tank. You can ride a long way before you run out of fuel.

Harley-Davidson V-Rod

Harley-Davidson launched the V-Rod in 2002. It's much lighter and faster than other Harley-Davidson bikes.

The V-Rod's fuel tank is under the seat. This leaves room for air intakes. Air intakes force air into the fuel tank. This drags in extra fuel. It gives the V-Rod more power.

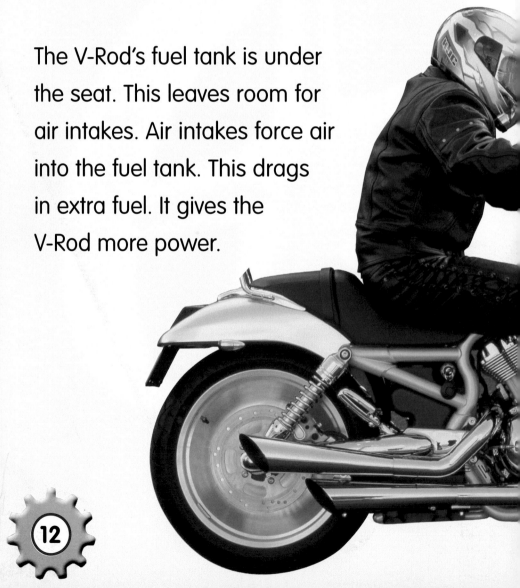

This badge shows that
Harley-Davidson has made
bikes since 1903.

Ducati 999S

There are three kinds of Ducati 999. The 999S has a top speed of over 274 km/h and can **accelerate** from 0 to 100 km/h in less than 3 seconds.

The Ducati 999S has won three world championships in superbike racing.

You can make the 999S more comfortable to ride. The seat and fuel tank move backwards and forwards. The footrests move up and down.

MV Agusta F4 SPR Senna

Ayrton Senna was a famous Formula One racing driver. He died in a race. The Senna motorcycle is named after him.

The twin **headlights** are stacked on top of each other.

MV Agusta only made 300 F4 SPR Sennas.

The Senna is a beautiful bike. It has a **streamlined** shape.

Suzuki GSX1300R Hayabusa

Suzuki launched the Hayabusa in 1998. It was the fastest road bike of its time. A hayabusa is a Japanese bird of prey.

The GSXR100 is the Hayabusa's little brother. It has better **acceleration** than the Hayabusa because it is lighter.

Suzuki GSXR1000

The Suzuki GSXR1000 is a very powerful racing bike. It is used in many superbike world championship races.

The Suzuki GSXR1000 is extremely light. Part of it is made of **titanium**.

The Suzuki GSXR1000 is so light, it can accelerate from 0 to 97 km/h in just under 2.5 seconds.

The top speed of the Suzuki GSXR1000 is 306 km/h!

Yamaha YZF-R1

Yamaha is famous for making motorcycles. The R1 can do 120 km/h in first **gear**. It can do over 160 km/h in second gear!

The YZF-R6 is one of Yamaha's most popular bikes. It isn't as fast as an R1 but it is small and light.

This is the Yamaha YZF-R1 2007. It can accelerate from 0 to 97 km/h in under 3 seconds. Its top speed is over 304 km/h!

Glossary

Acceleration Making a bike go faster.

Bodywork Part of bike that covers the engine and frame.

Engine Part of bike where fuel is burned to make more energy.

Exhaust Pipe at back of bike where gases escape.

Frame Part of bike that holds the engine, wheels and body together.

Gears Gears let a bike go faster or slower.

Headlight Bright light at front of bike.

Streamlined Smooth shape that helps bikes go faster.

Titanium A very hard, but very light metal.

Turbo-charged Turbo-charged means air is forced into the engine – this drags in fuel to make more power.